Skeleton of a Girl

Skeleton of a Girl

Amber Ashley Miller

Copyright © 2018 Amber Ashley Miller

All rights reserved.

ISBN-13: 978-0-692-03992-2

Instagram handle(s): @ambermiller_
and @askeletonofagirl

DEDICATION

Here's to the ones that left me helpless

And for the ones who didn't know

Here's to the ones who showed me kindness

And the ones who just let go

Here's to the ones that watched me crumble

And the ones that kept me intact

Here's to the girl that changed because of all of you

And here's to the girl you won't get back

CONTENTS

Acknowledgments

1   Heart

2   Flesh

3   Mind

4   Bones

About the Author

Love Letters to my Life

What's to come 🦋

ACKNOWLEDGMENTS

I first and foremost would like to say thank you from the deepest part of my soul to the beautiful and talented Michele Meek for making this book possible. Thank you for believing in me and my passion.

I would also like to thank Moises David Espinales, for illustrating my book and bringing it to life. I hope to collaborate with you again in the near future. You are amazingly talented, and I am honored to have your work be a reflection to my words.

I also want to thank my wonderful parents for always supporting me and loving me, especially through this incredibly exciting time in my journey.

Lastly thank you all who had a hand in this process. I love you all.

Heart

All of us are looking for someone

Something to stop the pain

I find a remedy in you

Coffee has a way of tattooing its taste on my lips

You and coffee have a lot in common

— It's not the coffee I crave it's the taste your lips convey

Envious of the sheets, that envelop you in your sleep

Perhaps I'm not impressed with the company you keep

You stained my lips

You imprinted your touch

There should be no surprise

Why I want you so much

I want to be your world

Not just part of it

— *My world revolves around you, is it the same for you*

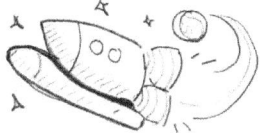

Ravish my belief

I sacrifice my mouth

Idle I leave my soul

Remorseful be thou

You spoke of sin

It melted on my lips

Forget not my devotion

Devour me

You may just be the moon

But I am the lowly tide

Hanging on your every move

Dear boy who lives amongst the stars

You left your shadow in my bed

So come quick and be here instead

Your lips are the oceans

And they are drowning me

I'm encased in your waves

Yet I don't want to be saved

I want to be stranded out at sea

I love you, how funny

If I am made of stars and you of the sea,

Then I would shine above every ocean

Just to set our love free

My heart has taken cover

My lips have asked for more

A wondrous contradiction

In my blood forevermore

I remember your arms, and how they felt around my waist

I'll never be satisfied with any other taste

Tell me we will be together soon

Just as the sun promised the moon

Why did life drift us apart

And leave us aching within our hearts

But maybe we will sail together once more and finally this

Distance will be brought to shore

— *J, R, S, E, L*

I keep you in sight

praying you won't let me go

But I fear late at night

More than you'll ever know

Your lips were so easy to get used to

And so hard to forget

— *Raspberry white mocha*

A constant ache a lingering crave

To be in your arms

To calm down your rage

I love you so that it might seem constricting

But I need you to know

You're always my something missing

The rain makes me think of you

Because it's falling hard

And I am too

You complain how you hate how women are acting

And I'm hating some men

Yet we sit together on a Sunday

And engage in pretend

I'm asking myself how much of this can I really take

We fake it like it's not love

We've been listening to too much Drake

Like the sand by the sea

I lay down and you got attached to me

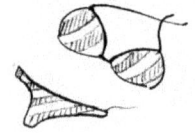

It was like I was missing some sort of fuel to my soul

One that was tailored by you and only for me to know

I wish things were easy and good from the start

Regardless of what happened

I love you from the bottom of my heart

You're the poem I continue to write

A constant uncertainty

That somehow makes me feel just right

You say you want a bad girl baby

Cause you think it'll be fun

But you're holding me at 2 am

So you fell in love with one

You have told me you loved me many times before

But last night when you said it

It meant much more

I don't know what made me fully believe you this time

You have become a resident and captivated my own mind

He was so much more than just a boy who broke my heart

He was the one that showed me what was missing

And gave my soul a jumpstart

You're under my skin

A pretty picture stored within

Even with all the power that you hold

You're the story I never told

I'd rather die in every way

And be rid of all that words can say

Than to live without you for one more day

And even though our chapter ended

Our story never did

And we will move as one

Like the wind affects the sea

Changes are frequent

But the constant is you and me

You smell like peanut butter, hopes, and dreams

    — to the cutest little man in all of the land

And I hope you remember my taste

Even when you no longer remember my face

— *bubble mint*

We all become stories that we tell when we're old

Of lovers that we lost and ones we still hold

And what will you be when I'm old and I'm grey

Will you be fearless by my side

Or will I be wishing you had stayed

— A.A.O

Wait for the one…

Who makes you smile on your worst day,

Despite your flaws chooses to stay,

And says I love you in a hundred ways

But what if you aren't just a poem in my book

What if you're the reason I'm still writing

I once knew a man

Who hid behind his pain

He was there for them all

But he shielded them from his shame

I once knew a girl

Who hid behind her heart

She had love for them all

But they tore her apart

Soul mates

Flesh

And I miss our midnight kisses

That tasted like bitter goodbyes

When you held me at 2 am I broke down and I cried

Now I'm left with your scent

And hand me down memories

Alone without touch

And the deafening sound of needing you

Oh sweet ghost of you

Be alive with me soon

Your words mislead

Your mind stays jumbled

I obeyed your creed

But you allowed me to stumble

You attempted to make me slip

With your words that flattered

But when you released your grip

You showed me that in your eyes

You were all that mattered

— *The Capricorn*

My soul is in the endless wreck of autumn

My life brings forth life and death

But all the while it remains beautiful

All shades of sadness are the beauty my sorrow creates

In all they bring to me a new happiness

But I am left tattered and broken

Between what was and what is to come

Love ends, people change, and time never looks back

But I unlike time always look back

I look back at the storms I've created

And the waves I've tried to calm

I look back at the stains I've made

And the wounds I've caused

I unlike time, own up to what I have done

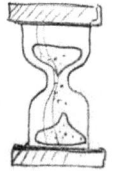

You placed a gun to my head

And you didn't hesitate to pull the trigger

The sickest part is I would give anything

To feel your hand pressed against my head again

So if you tell me you love me don't expect me to believe

Cause I'll be the one broken

When you change your mind and leave

— *Love picks you up, love stays*

I find a strange comfort

In the agony of missing you

I cried myself to sleep

I cried myself awake

I'm tired of talking to you

Through these damp and tattered pages

I know that smile

It's the smile that is unaware

Of what happens when he leaves

I remember that smile

It's the smile I used to have when he was mine

Our love

And our loss

Became a beautiful poem

But nothing more

— To the one I said forever to

Lets mix our poison

Different yet the same

Infect my mind

And drive me insane

I'm always expecting for this time to be different

And when it turns out to be exactly the same

My body stalls and there is an excruciating pain

All of a sudden it feels like too much

Why do I crumble with only a touch

It's always the bad ones

That taste the sweetest

And hurt the most

What do I do now that your scent is gone

From all the old t-shirts you left?

Is it still okay to wear your old sweater?

Even if you're not mine anymore

And it serves no use in this weather

Whenever I pick up your scent I always stop

And close my eyes and picture you right next to me

But when I open my eyes I'm hit by my painful reality

You're not really here and you're not even mine

And it even makes me doubt if you once ever were

I want the first kiss

The first time we touched

I want that back

So fucking much

The sound of your voice and whispers through your lips

The amazing touch by your fingertips

My heart is forever fractured by those words you uttered

That left me alone with only a stutter

I crave for the day you say you were wrong

So hear my cry and meditate on my song

It must be nice to get to know the deepest parts of him

It must be nice to get late night calls from him

It must be nice to have his trust and a hold on to him

It must be nice to be able to love him

It must be nice to not have to try to forget him

We were always smiling in

Old photographs and home videos

But never in real time behind closed doors

But yet I'm sitting here looking back

Convincing myself that we were happy

Why does a broken heart blind you from reality?

I feel you in my soul

Inciting chaos, no control

Here you are residing in my deepest parts

Composing pain like a work of art

Mi querido perdido

te extraño

I don't understand why I pick up for you still

When you leave me feeling empty

As I bend to your will

It feels as if I've missed you all this time

And I'm in so much pain

Because you still aren't mine

Around you my feelings seem to run and hide

Because revealing my hand seems to be unwise

Two of the same, too stubborn to admit

So how can I love you if we can't even commit

— *To my scorpion*

I gasped for air

But you were no longer there

You are not special to him,

"love" he's incapable of that

But he will tell you those three words

So suddenly you're trapped

It's a shot in the dark

I'm screaming with no air

And you always say you love me

When you know I'm not there

I want a love that feels like fall

But instead I'm left like the trees

With nothing at all

You are my greatest disaster

— *I'm just trying to survive you*

I always feel lost

Like I'm longing to be found

So what will it cost

To be picked up from the ground

He is the sun and I am the moon

As much as we want to shine together

We can't

I'm tired of being the butterfly

Who is cursed with a broken wing

Why can't I be as courageous

As the hummingbird who lives to sing

And maybe you message me out of the blue

Just to see if I'm hanging on

But I'll give you what you are seeking

Because I'm always going to respond

I guess part of me never really gave up on you

Even if I really should

But maybe you'll see I love you

And the fact that I always did

Your taste is one I savored

Now I crave to forget

And even though we don't talk anymore

I hope you're doing alright

I can't stop myself from thinking about you

On every sleepless night

You may not be flooded with thoughts of me

Or wasting precious time

But a part of me will always wait for you

And that's my thankless crime

You told me your favorite songs

And the funniest things you've ever heard

I listened to you speak and I meditated on every word

And when you stopped

And asked me I didn't know what to do

I was caught off guard

Cause my favorite things are anything

And everything to do with you

As time goes on

I wonder if my mind has made you seem kinder

Than you were

                        But I can't discredit all the storms inside me

                                That you continue to stir

Your name rolls so easily off my tongue

Like a record overplayed

And maybe if I felt like her

Maybe you would have stayed

— *How do I stop loving you?*

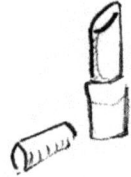

And while you're out with another

Spitting words you don't mean

Just remember how I held you

When you were split at the seam

You broke me

While I was building you

Mind

Not throwing away my heart....

I think of love so much it feels just like telepathy

When's it going to come for me

Off my seat, clenching to its melody

If I see it pass do I run for it or do I let it seize

Is it like a dream without the ending?

Cause I always thought I would have it past twenty

Where I come from only some get it in plenty

*— Inspired by Hamilton the Musical
by Lin Manuel Miranda*

The girl I once was is such a stranger to me

I wish I could save her from the things she could not see

Sometimes I envy her ignorant bliss

Although it managed to cover her hollowness

I'm still searching for the things that were lost

But I don't know if I'm prepared to pay the cost

Hunger will lead to beauty

And pain is the price to pay

I was misled to believe that this is the only way

Seduce my mind

My body is already yours

Roses are beautiful and crash when they fall

But a prick on the finger makes no sound at all

All the monsters have gone away

But I will allow for one to stay

A misspelled word

a broken clock

a loud cry

a breath when you talk

a wake up call

a break from the fall

it leaves you stranded with nothing at all

you shake off the rubble

and arise from the sand

you see what you've done

the blood on your hand

you see what you caused

but never intended

you see the broken heart

you could have mended

your eyes are left cold and hard

you try to look in the mirror to remember who you are

your eyes become drenched

with the pain of the past

it could have all been prevented

but no it could not last

now he is gone

he's in the past

Scared to lose

Terrified to win

If a good girl loves a bad boy

And an angel loves the devil

Is it cosmic balance?

Or the world's demise?

Kill your mind

Inhabit mine

If selfies told the story that we hold within

No one would take them

In fear of exposing our sin

'

The promises you speak are elusive and compelling

But do you even believe all the lies that you're telling?

In regards to you

Am I a somebody

Or just a body to use

I always think the people to count on

Are the sirens that sing the sweetest

But when you slip into their trance you realize

They are the meanest

Please don't get confused they are only concerned

With what girl looks the leanest

I hope you see this

— *I'm delusional*

I come alive at night

When the pain turns to numbness

And I finally feel alright

I'm humanizing my demons

Suddenly they speak with reason

Her eyes dripped of honey

        And her touch always seemed to sting

I'm trying to find love in all the wrong places

Just to feel safe with familiar faces

I'm giving up on real love

'Cause it feels like it's a response

That is never good enough

It doesn't seem real to me

But there was a time that all I did was believe

I've become okay with mediocrity

Something that's close to what I want

But isn't what it turns out to be

It's like closing your eyes but still claiming to see

I'm pushing down all my feelings and hiding the true me

You want perfection but look at yourself

You're going around calling girls fake for being themselves

Thank you for your fake sincerity

You brought your lies to the feet of clarity

I don't need your apology or the touch of a friend

I just need to get back to my old self

And fix the messages I send

I'm so concerned with what others think

And as soon as I get grasp of one idea it's gone in a blink

It's like there are millions of versions of what others see

And it's all I am concerned with

I've forgotten how to be me

It seems as if you have fun wasting time

And I'm giving you all the power to do so with mine

Let me mourn you like a death

So I can slowly bring ease to my heart

And give my mind a rest

Life is tough and boys are shitty

So we roam around and search

For answers in different cities

I wish life were as beautiful

As the pictures we capture

'Cause each passing day

I'm in search for that happily ever after

I feel so much

I feel nothing at all

You draw women into your morgue

Life is all around you

But you radiate nothing but death

Pick your poison

And stick to what you claim

And maybe it will be what you're used to

Just with a different name

And I will never forget what that young woman said

"How can we appreciate flowers from loved ones

When we only receive them when we're dead"

Bones

You have fed off of my parts

There is nothing left to take

I've become a skeleton of a girl

That no one can break

This is my fire let me walk through it

And some parts of us are meant to die

In order to leave room

For pieces to come together

To give the new a chance to bloom

Yet I'm still holding on

To this lengthy ideal

That so much beauty

Will soon come

From all this pain that I feel

I am the moon to lead her way

Her path is darkened by what others say

When others discourage and deflate her wings

I move the tides to help her sing

She's beauty and love in all the right ways

But others words seem to make her fray

Her tattered heart is pure to see

From where others tore and left her for me

Don't worry skeleton girl you're about to be free

— The ballad of the moon

Be the real

Amongst the false

I can't wait to come alive again

Please don't let them make you feel small

Believe me when I say you're beautiful

Stand up tall

That good feeling you crave

Will come and find its way

Once I started loving myself

I began to have no room to love someone

Who didn't love me in the way that I needed

Once you find your self-worth

You begin to see who is worthy of taking up space

— *You are a goddess*

You are radiant and unstoppable

Don't let people define you

They are incapable

I wish you saw all the beauty you hold

And ignored all the mean things you have ever been told

Even though you see the truth as a lie

I wish you would listen or at least say you'd try

I hope these words resonate in your bones

So that one day you can feel all the beauty that is shown.

— *The one who is blind*

I've never been impressed

With what others could give me

I can do it for myself

My success will be self-inflicting

You can't be everyone's damsel in distress

Not every relationship you're in

Is guaranteed a happily ever after

All my life I've been told I'm too much

too sensitive

too weak

too tall

too skinny

too fat

too weird

too fake

too cocky

too ugly

too dramatic

too loud

too much

And it took 21 years to realize how much value I'm putting into what the world thinks of me. I may be too much of all these things.

But to all who put these disgusting painful thoughts in my head and to those who allowed me to carry them.

I just wanted to tell you that you were right.

I am too much.

And as a matter of fact,

I'm way too much for you.

We have all become products

Of whatever social media breathes

We have bought into the lie that this is all we can be

We continue to compare and conform to the new trend

There's no telling when this madness

Will finally come to an end

This false alternate universe is doing more harm than good

Young girls are thinking they aren't beautiful

Like they should

Now I'm not saying I'm above it not even close

Matter of fact it's killing me too I don't mean to impose

I am just trying to express how it's been making me feel

Shook out of my own reality now

I don't know what's even real

I know we are all worth so much more

And I hope everyone can one day

Find what they been yearning for

You were very quick to tear me down with just one word

But soon enough you're going to regret

The line you blurred

I'll make you suffocate on the claim that you made

Fortunately my strength isn't something I can trade

But I can assure you, you will never be someone to me

Because you spit on me when I was down

Next time think more carefully

Don't allow his sweet nothings implement your mind

You think about them so much

You make excuses for less than kind

I know it's hard to swallow

But there is nothing to gain from him

Take a deep breath and walk away

That's the only way you can win

You may be the sun that radiates heat

But I am the moon that will thrive on every retreat

Turns out I don't need you to feel whole

I am the only one with the power

To bring healing to my soul

You're intoxicating baby

But you've been so toxic to yourself

My heart is restless because the last remains

Of a lover have been shed

So I begged my head to tell my heart

To love myself instead

I don't need a savior

I'm a survivor

I'm nothing that you've ever seen

Take it or leave it

For I am composed of two extremes

Be selfish

Self sufficient

Self-empowering

Self lusting

Society doesn't define you

His decisions are not a reflection of you

Being loved by someone doesn't complete you

Achieving wholeness is only something you can do

You deserve someone

That chooses you

— *Say this over and over until you believe it*

When I was 21 I realized there was one person in my life

Who truly taught me how to love me for me

So here's to you

The one who loved me enough

To set me free

She burned like the sun

And she shined like it too

It was hard to compare her

Even harder to outdo

                                              She was cold like the moon

                                                 But she shined like it too

                                                 It was hard to compare her

                                                     Even harder to outdo

Acknowledge the pain

Let it consume you

Let it drown you

Then let it go

— I do this more than you'll ever know

I promised you a poem

And I am not sure where to start

You came into my life so soon

I cannot imagine a time we were apart

You never fail to be my strength

You never fail to show how much you care

You're the hero to the story

You are the half of me that was always there

This one is for you

Even though you deserve more than words and a hook

Dear my very best friend

You're the ending to my book

— *To my sister*

ABOUT THE AUTHOR

After experiencing heartbreak for the first time, Amber found poetry as a means to cope and process grief. After many years of struggling with feeling inadequate, Amber realized that she could use her gift for writing poetry as an outlet for her pain. When you read these poems, you will see how more often than not pain can be delivered by the hands of those closest to us. We hope that you realize the power of love and the destruction that lives in our tongues, which can produce whispers of light or darkness. This should strike a question within our hearts, which do we want to be the sender and receiver of? Amber believes that there is strength in weakness and beauty within pain, and the true struggle lies within the perception of ourselves. Amber would like to encourage all those struggling souls that are scarred from within to rise above limitations, especially the ones others have placed on us.

A message from the future….

A lot has changed, yet some stayed the same.

The heart does heal, even after excruciating pain.

You are happy and whole.

You are in love with an extraordinary man,

most importantly you fell in love with you….

If you want to know if things worked out okay,

I am living proof.

There is love, strength and happiness waiting just for you.

Love letters to my life.
& a preview of what is to come.

2022

New York, November 2022. The magic it holds.

Your body and soul hold so much power..

Reciprocate the love the mirror has shown you. It is your eyes that needs changing.

This girl has grown and overcome so much.

embrace her.

Love of my life. You were worth the wait.

You are a goddess. Thrive

This night ended in tears. If only you saw your beauty.

*This is not the end, **Mariposa**.*
See you soon.